P9-CLJ-380

MAKING THE PLAY

FOOTBALL

BY VALERIE BODDEN

CREATIVE EDUCATION • CREATIVE PAPERBACKS

Published by Creative Education and Creative Paperbacks
P.O. Box 227, Mankato, Minnesota 56002
Creative Education and Creative Paperbacks
are imprints of The Creative Company
www.thecreativecompany.us

Design and production by The Design Lab
Art direction by Rita Marshall
Printed in the United States of America

Photographs by Dreamstime (James Boardman),
iStockphoto (Jason Lugo, OSTILL, t_kimura, zakazpc),
Shutterstock (Aspen Photo, EKS, eurobanks, ostill, Pete
Saloutos, Carlos E. Santa Maria), Thinkstock (OSTILL)

Library of Congress Cataloging-in-Publication Data
Bodden, Valerie.
Football / Valerie Bodden.
p. cm. — (Making the play)
Includes index.
Summary: An elementary introduction to the physics involved in
the sport of football, including scientific concepts such as mass
and projectile motion, and actions such as tackling and punting.
ISBN 978-1-60818-655-6 (hardcover)
ISBN 978-1-62832-234-7 (pbk)
ISBN 978-1-56660-686-8 (eBook)
I. Football—Juvenile literature. 2. Physics—Juvenile literature. I. Title.

GV950.7.B64 2016
796.332—dc23   2015007577

CCSS: RI.I.I, 2, 3, 4, 5, 6, 7; RI.2.I, 2, 3, 5, 6, 7,
I0; RI.3.I, 3, 5, 7, 8; RF.2.3, 4; RF.3.3

First Edition HC 9 8 7 6 5 4 3 2 I
First Edition PBK 9 8 7 6 5 4 3 2 I

CONTENTS

FOOTBALL AND SCIENCE

You tuck the football under your arm.

You pass the other players. You dash

into the end zone. Touchdown!

TOUCHDOWN!

Do you think about science when you play football? Probably not. But you use science anyway. A science called physics (*FIZ-icks*) can help you hit, kick, and throw. Let's see how!

CENTER OF MASS

Football players stay low to the ground. This lowers their center of **mass**. Having a low center of mass makes it easier to balance.

CENTER OF MASS

The midpoint of a body from which it can be balanced

CENTER OF MASS

Try to hold a pencil on your fingertip. The spot where the pencil rests without falling off is its center of mass. A person's center of mass is near the belly button.

It is easier to tackle someone below his center of mass. This is why a football player stays low.

13

UP-AND-DOWN MOTION

A moving football is a **projectile**. It moves

forward and up until gravity pulls it down.

GRAVITY

A force that pulls
all objects toward
the earth

A projectile curves through the air. It goes up to its highest point. Then it comes back down. It looks like a spray of water.

Punters kick the ball high. That makes it stay in the air longer. But it will not go as far. How can you use projectile motion to throw a pass? Give it a try, and make the play!

OBJECTS ON THE MOVE

You can use projectile motion to make an object travel farther or stay in the air longer.

WHAT YOU NEED

- Garden hose
- Tape measure
- A friend

Point the hose straight in front of you. Turn on the faucet. Have your friend measure the distance to the spot where the water lands. Point the hose higher as you repeat these steps a few more times. Which hose position made the water travel farthest? Which position made the water stay in the air longest? What does that tell you about projectile motion?

GLOSSARY

mass-the amount of material that makes up an object

projectile-something shot, thrown, or launched through the air

punters-people on a football team who kick the ball

READ MORE

Gore, Bryson. *Physics*. Mankato, Minn.: Stargazer, 2009.

McClellan, Ray. *Football*. Minneapolis: Bellwether Media, 2010.

Walton, Ruth. *Let's Go to the Playground*. Mankato, Minn.: Sea-to-Sea, 2013.

WEBSITES

NBC Learn: Science of NFL Football
https://www.nbclearn.com/portal /site/learn/science-of-nfl-football
Check out these videos to see where else you can find science in football.

Study Jams! Gravity & Inertia
http://studyjams.scholastic.com /studyjams/jams/science /forces-and-motion /fgravity-and-inertia.htm
Watch a video to learn more about how gravity works.

NOTE: Every effort has been made to ensure that the websites listed above are suitable for children, that they have educational value, and that they contain no inappropriate material. However, because of the nature of the Internet, it is impossible to guarantee that these sites will remain active indefinitely or that their contents will not be altered.

INDEX